ACCENTS OF

GOD

SELECTIONS FROM THE
WORLD'S SACRED SCRIPTURES

EDITED BY

M.K. ROHANI

ONEWORLD

OXFORD

Accents of God

Oneworld Publications Ltd
185 Banbury Road, Oxford, OX2 7AR, England

© Oneworld Publications Ltd 1991
All rights reserved.
Copyright under Berne Convention
A CIP record for this book is available from the
British Library

ISBN 1-85168-023-3

Printed in Great Britain at the Alden Press, Oxford

ACCENTS OF

GOD

By the same author

Contemplating Life's Greatest Questions
Contemplating a Spiritual Life (forthcoming)

Through their appearance the revelation of God is made manifest, and by their countenance the Beauty of God is revealed. Thus it is that the accents of God Himself have been heard uttered by these Manifestations of the divine Being.

-- BAHÁ'U'LLÁH

INTRODUCTION

———

All through history people have longed to know the meaning of life, to find a happiness immune to life's anxieties that is not subject to the passage of time and which transcends the inevitability and finality of death. It is this longing that religion promises to fulfil and, everywhere in the world, some form of religion has always existed, mapping out a route to this end. Whether it be from a tribal religion in South America or a world religion such as Islam, there has always been a voice pointing us beyond the temporal to the eternal.

Accents of God briefly examines six different world religions, their common basis and how they seek to help us attain what they themselves present as the ultimate goal of life. This book contains a single selection from the primary Scriptures of Hinduism, Judaism, Buddhism, Christianity, Islam and the Bahá'í Faith. All of these selections allow us to see how religion has provided spiritual guidance from very ancient times, as with Hinduism and Judaism, up to more recent history with Islam and the Bahá'í Faith.

Each of these religious traditions has its own distinctive form of expression that reflects its cultural and historical setting. Nevertheless, they all hold in common certain essential teachings with regard to the nature, meaning and purpose of life. Primarily, there are three themes intrinsic to each of these great religions. First, they all teach that there is an eternal changeless reality that transcends the temporal and limited world of everyday existence. Second, each asserts that this eternal reality is within the grasp of us all – all human beings can acquire the eternal and divine attributes of love, patience, detachment, forgiveness and so on, and thereby attain to a peace that enables us to overcome the difficulties of this life. Third, they all affirm that the attainment of this reality is both the purpose of our existence and the way to true happiness. All religions have expounded on these basic principles in some form and have provided a way to achieve this ultimate and eternal goal.

On a practical level, there are essentially two ways in which these religions have sought to provide us with a path to this goal.

The first is the devotional path centred on the original proponent or figurehead of the religion, such as Krishna, Buddha, Christ and Bahá'u'lláh, or on the ultimate symbol of the divine that He represents, such as God or the Supreme Brahman. Through prayer and devotion to this Source of enlightenment and Symbol of the ultimate goal, the believer or devotee develops a more focused and spiritually centred life. The other, closely associated with this devotional path, is a series of laws and principles by which good relations are established between people, thus bringing the divine qualities of the eternal reality into everyday human experience.

In all of these religions, the path is conveyed or transmitted from generation to generation in the form of Scripture and tradition. Such sacred writings have existed since ancient times, exerting an immense influence on the way people lived and understood life. In some cases, these writings or Scriptures are derived from an even more ancient oral tradition.

The further we go back the more difficult it is to ascertain the objective facts or dates of these religious traditions. With the appearance of Buddha, Christ, Muḥammad and even more recently, Bahá'u'lláh, historical and circumstantial details gradually become clearer and the reliability of religious texts more certain. Nevertheless, it can be argued that Scripture is not ultimately concerned with the recording of historical facts; its focus is primarily the spiritual dimension of life, and particularly those qualities of life that enable us to transcend the mundane and the temporal. In the oldest Scriptures, this spirit has survived the perils of history and the insecurities of transmission. The meaning of some details may have become lost or distorted but, as we will see, the dominant theme of the eternal and our relationship to it remains vibrant, compelling and very real.

Today people read Scripture for a variety of reasons. Some scholars, for example, are primarily interested in its cultural or historical merits. These aspects are admittedly interesting in and of themselves but, if we are studying Scripture from a religious point of view, it is these very cultural aspects that can obscure the spiritual answers we are seeking or, at least, make the search more difficult. This is due, in part, to the fact that we inevitably judge Scripture according to our own experience and knowledge. For example, the laws and practices described in the more ancient Scriptures, such as those of the Hindus and Jews, are difficult for many people to understand in the twentieth century. While some are clearly inappropriate for the needs of today, our objections may not always be well placed. We find, for instance, that many Christians in recent times have objected to Muḥammad's apparent acceptance of polygamy and military force, yet the same practices were sanctioned and practised in Old Testament times, Scriptures that Christians have traditionally regarded as the Word of God. During Muḥammad's day no one criticized Him for the reasons offered today. While some of His legal and social principles seem primitive to us now, they were instrumental in raising up a highly cultivated civilization vastly superior, in its day, to any in Europe. Furthermore, certain of Muḥammad's teachings, in particular those about God, inspired some of humanity's highest and most evolved mystical thought.

Each religious tradition has teachings that pertain to its particular age and teachings that pertain to the eternal mysteries, unbound by time or place. Naturally there will always be some things that will be hard for us to understand, but if we can focus on the eternal elements that are not limited by cultural traits, we can find much that the religions hold in common and much from which we all can benefit. There can be no doubt as to the power of the religious experience that has helped these Scriptures survive and exert such an enduring influence on human affairs.

Some will argue that religion has done as much harm as good. However, when we look at those human ideologies, particularly the self-confessedly anti-religious ones, that have been put into practice, it is apparent that such criticism fails to consider how much worse conditions might have been in the absence of any religious restraints. Moreover, it is not valid to blame religion for the damage caused by those who have misused it or to judge it on the basis of antagonisms it has expressly sought to subdue; the religious experience is too personal to be dismissed because of errors committed by some believers in the course of history. The materialism of modern life, which has given rise to so much indifference to religion, has offered no substantive alternative that can satisfy our deepest spiritual longings. The questions, mysteries and difficulties of life still remain with us. For as long as people seek to know the meaning and purpose of life and reach out for peace within themselves, we can expect these Scriptures to endure.

H I N D U I S M

———

The Bhagavad-gītā comes to us from the sub-continent of India which has a long and diverse religious tradition usually referred to as Hinduism. Hinduism is a complex system of beliefs often difficult to define. As knowledge about it grows in the West, earlier views are being discarded. Some now argue that many of the sects of Hinduism are so different that it can no longer be regarded either as a single religion or as a polytheistic Faith, as was once believed.* It has no single founder and its literature is vast, dating from different historical periods and finding different degrees of acceptance amongst Hindus. Nevertheless, within the Indian religious tradition certain texts have gained widespread acceptance. Among these is the Bhagavad-gītā.

The Bhagavad-gītā has been regarded by some as the essence of all other Scriptures. It has inspired countless commentaries and, like Jesus' Sermon on the Mount, has been translated into every major language, in some cases numerous times. After translations began to circulate in English, it quickly gained a popularity of its own in the Western world.

The Bhagavad-gītā, which means the 'Song of God', or 'Song of the Glorious One', is actually a relatively small section of a larger epic known as the Mahābhārata. However, some believe it may have been an independent work inserted in this classic epic at a later time. It is generally believed to date back at least as far as 400-100 BC, but some argue that its actual origins are much older.

Scholars are also uncertain about the authorship of the text, but tradition attributes the present version to Vyāsa, whose name simply means 'the Arranger'. Nevertheless, the inspiration and knowledge it contains is attributed to Krishna, who is said to be a manifestation in human form, or incarnation, of the Supreme Brahman, God. For this reason the text is regarded by many followers of Krishna as an authoritative and infallible revelation.

Its contents recount a dialogue between a warrior named Arjuna and the Lord Krishna, who has in this instance manifested

* See Hans Küng, *Christianity and the World Religions* 138.

Himself as Arjuna's chariot driver. The setting is an open plain on the eve of a great battle between the Pāṇḍavas and their cousins the Kauravas. This may have been a true historical event around 1000 BC. The warrior, Arjuna, is torn between fighting for a cause he regards as just, and the knowledge that he will have to fight many of his own family and relations who are on the other side. Troubled by this conflict he turns to his friend Krishna for advice. What follows is Krishna's explanation of the meaning of existence, the nature of divine reality, and the different ways to attain the highest spiritual goal.

Some interpreters have regarded the battle to be a metaphor for the battle between the forces of good and evil within us, the struggle for spiritual enlightenment and salvation. Arjuna's relatives represent our attachments to this world and the battle is the necessary struggle we must wage against these attachments in order to attain spiritual self-mastery. The instructions Krishna delivers are intended to tell us how we can succeed in this struggle.

It is not easy to take any one chapter of the Bhagavad-gītā in isolation from the rest. The overall text itself is short and each chapter is related to the others while embodying significant and profound truths. Nevertheless, in chapters nine and ten, mid-way through the work, we find the text expounding on the central goal of the spiritual life - attainment to the divine reality - which is here expressed in the person of Krishna. This reality is the source and essence of salvation and hence is central to the message of the Bhagavad-gītā. Indeed, it is so important that Krishna tells Arjuna in an earlier passage how, in order to offer this grace to humankind, He has, out of His compassion, appeared in every age:

> For protection of the good,
> And the destruction of evil–doers,
> To make a firm footing for the right,
> I come into being in age after age. (4:8)

Krishna also delineates the different ways people have worshipped God, but eventually sets forth the path of devotion to Him (Bhakti) as the supreme way to attain to the divine Presence. This is essentially the mystical path of the love of God.

✷

The Supreme Lord said:

My dear Arjuna, because you are never envious of Me, I shall impart to you this most secret wisdom, knowing which you shall be relieved of the miseries of material existence.

This knowledge is the king of education, the most secret of all secrets. It is the purest knowledge, and because it gives direct perception of the self by realization, it is the perfection of religion. It is everlasting, and it is joyfully performed.

Those who are not faithful on the path of devotional service* cannot attain Me, O conqueror of foes, but return to birth and death in this material world.

By Me, in My unmanifested form, this entire universe is pervaded. All beings are in Me, but I am not in them.

And yet everything that is created does not rest in Me. Behold My mystic opulence! Although I am the maintainer of all living entities, and although I am everywhere, still My Self is the very source of creation.

---

* The term 'dharma' or 'dharmasya' is here translated as 'the path of devotional service' which expresses the intended meaning well. The 'dharma' is essentially the sacred or spiritual 'law' that governs the universe as well as the religious and moral law that Krishna and later Buddha urge people to abide by.

As the mighty wind, blowing everywhere, always rests in ethereal space, know that in the same manner all beings rest in Me.

O son of Kunti*, at the end of the millennium every material manifestation enters into My nature, and at the beginning of another millennium, by My potency I again create.

The whole cosmic order is under Me. By My will it is manifested again and again, and by My will it is annihilated at the end.

O Dhanañjaya, all this work cannot bind Me. I am ever detached, seated as though neutral.

This material nature is working under My direction, O son of Kuntī, and it is producing all moving and unmoving beings. By its rule this manifestation is created and annihilated again and again.

Fools deride Me when I descend in the human form. They do not know My transcendental nature and My supreme dominion over all that be.

Those who are thus bewildered are attracted by demonic and atheistic views. In that deluded condition, their hopes for liberation, their fruitive activities, and their culture of knowledge are all defeated.

O son of Pṛthā, those who are not deluded, the great souls, are under the protection of the divine nature. They are fully engaged in devotional service because they know Me as the Supreme Personality of Godhead, original and inexhaustible.

Always chanting My glories, endeavouring with great determination, bowing down before Me, these great souls perpetually worship Me with devotion.

* A reference to Arjuna's lineage through his mother.

Others, who are engaged in the cultivation of knowledge, worship the Supreme Lord as the one without a second, diverse in many, and in the universal form.

But it is I who am the ritual, I the sacrifice, the offering to the ancestors, the healing herb, the transcendental chant. I am the butter and the fire and the offering.

I am the father of this universe, the mother, the support, and the grandsire. I am the object of knowledge, the purifier and the syllable om. I am also the Ṛk, the Sāma, the Yajur [Vedas]*.

I am the goal, the sustainer, the master, the witness, the abode, the refuge and the most dear friend. I am the creation and the annihilation, the basis of everything, the resting place and the eternal seed.

O Arjuna, I control heat, the rain and the drought. I am immortality, and I am also death personified. Both being and non-being are in Me.

Those who study the Vedas and drink the soma juice, seeking the heavenly planets, worship Me indirectly. They take birth on the planet of Indra, where they enjoy godly delights.

When they have thus enjoyed heavenly sense pleasure, they return to this mortal planet again.§ Thus, through the Vedic principles, they achieve only flickering happiness.

---

* These are sacred syllables found in the hymns of the central Hindu texts known as the Vedas. The point appears to be that all the Vedas aim essentially towards the reality of Krishna.

§ References to rebirth are generally interpreted literally, as in the doctrine of reincarnation. However, this may well be metaphorical of successive attempts to realize one's true spiritual nature even while in this life. To be free from rebirth is to attain the ideal state of steadfastness in devotion to God.

But those who worship Me with devotion, meditating on My transcendental form – to them I carry what they lack and preserve what they have.

Whatever a man may sacrifice to other gods, O son of Kunti, is really meant for Me alone, but it is offered without true understanding.

I am the only enjoyer and the only object of sacrifice. Those who do not recognize My true transcendental nature fall down.

Those who worship the demigods will take birth among the demigods; those who worship ghosts and spirits will take birth among such beings; those who worship ancestors go to the ancestors; and those who worship Me will live with Me.

If one offers Me with love and devotion a leaf, a flower, fruit or water, I will accept it.

O son of Kunti, all that you do, all that you eat, all that you offer and give away, as well as all austerities that you may perform, should be done as an offering unto Me.

In this way you will be freed from all reactions to good and evil deeds, and by this principle of renunciation you will be liberated and come to Me.

I envy no one, nor am I partial to anyone. I am equal to all. But whoever renders service unto Me in devotion is a friend, is in Me, and I am also a friend to him.

Even if one commits the most abominable actions, if he is engaged in devotional service, he is to be considered saintly because he is properly situated.

He quickly becomes righteous and attains lasting peace. O son of Kunti, declare it boldly that My devotee never perishes.

O son of Pṛthā, those who take shelter in Me, though they be of lower birth – women*, vaiśyas [merchants], as well as śūdras [workers] – can approach the supreme destination.

How much greater then are the brāhmanas, the righteous, the devotees and saintly kings who in this temporary miserable world engage in loving service unto Me.

Engage your mind always in thinking of Me, offer obeisances and worship Me. Being completely absorbed in Me, surely you will come to Me.

The Supreme Lord said:

My dear friend, mighty-armed Arjuna, listen again to My supreme word, which I shall impart to you for your benefit and which will give you great joy.

Neither the hosts of demigods nor the great sages know My origin, for, in every respect, I am the source of the demigods and the sages.

He who knows Me as the unborn, as the beginningless, as the Supreme Lord of all the worlds – he, undeluded among men, is freed from all sins.

---

* This reference to women being of lower birth reflects the value placed on physical strength in more ancient cultures. This was responsible for the mostly male-dominated social hierarchies that have persisted through the ages. Krishna is not necessarily endorsing such values although it is likely that when the Bhagavad-gītā was written such hierarchical structures were seen as unavoidable if not essential for survival. Krishna obviously places higher value on the devotional and spiritual life and it is in this context that He is assuring those who are regarded as inferior that they are one in His sight and may attain the highest goal.

Intelligence, knowledge, freedom from doubt and delusion, forgiveness, truthfulness, self-control and calmness, pleasure and pain, birth, death, fear, fearlessness, non-violence, equanimity, satisfaction, austerity, charity, fame and infamy are created by Me alone.

The seven great sages and before them the four other great sages and the Manus [progenitors of mankind] are born out of My mind, and all creatures in these planets descend from them.

He who knows in truth this glory and power of Mine engages in unalloyed devotional service; of this there is no doubt.

I am the source of all spiritual and material worlds. Everything emanates from Me. The wise who know this perfectly engage in My devotional service and worship Me with all their hearts.

The thoughts of My pure devotees dwell in Me, their lives are surrendered to Me, and they derive great satisfaction and bliss enlightening one another and conversing about Me.

To those who are constantly devoted and worship Me with love, I give the understanding by which they can come to Me.

Out of compassion for them, I, dwelling in their hearts, destroy with the shining lamp of knowledge the darkness born of ignorance.

Arjuna said:

You are the Supreme Brahman, the ultimate, the supreme abode and purifier, the Absolute Truth and the eternal divine person. You are the primal God, transcendental and original, and You are the unborn and all-pervading beauty. All the great sages such as

Nārada, Asita, Devala, and Vyāsa proclaim this of you, and now You Yourself are declaring it to me.

O Kṛṣṇa [Krishna], I totally accept as truth all that You have told me. Neither the gods nor demons, O Lord, know Thy personality.

Indeed, You alone know Yourself by Your own potencies, O origin of all, Lord of all beings, God of gods, O Supreme Person, Lord of the universe!

Please tell me in detail of Your divine powers by which You pervade all these worlds and abide in them.

How should I meditate on You? In what various forms are You to be contemplated, O Blessed Lord?

Tell me again in detail, O Janārdana [Krishna], of Your mighty potencies and glories, for I never tire of hearing Your ambrosial words.

The Blessed Lord said:

Yes, I will tell you of My splendorous manifestations, but only of those which are prominent, O Arjuna, for My opulence is limitless.*

* Throughout the following verses of this chapter Krishna expounds on the nature of His divine attributes by making metaphorical equations to the greatest things known in creation. Because of the cultural context of the Bhagavad-gītā, the text employs references to places, objects, and other subjects familiar to Hindu literature but which are often little known to peoples of the West, especially by the Sanskrit names, such as Ādityas, Śankara and so on. Nevertheless, the purport of the text is apparent: the greatest of all that is attributable to Him is like a reflection, a mere indication of His infinite and exalted being. By using comparisons Krishna is providing a means of understanding the true divinity of the Godhead, which is otherwise entirely beyond comprehension.

I am the Self, O Guḍākesa, seated in the hearts of all creatures. I am the beginning, the middle and the end of all beings.

Of the Ādityas I am Viṣṇu, of lights I am the radiant sun, I am Marīci of the Maruts, and among the stars I am the moon.

Of the Vedas I am the Sāma-veda; of the demigods I am Indra; of the senses I am the mind, and in living beings I am the living force [knowledge].

Of all the Rudras I am Lord Śiva; of the Yakṣas and Rākṣasas I am the lord of wealth [Kuvera]; of the Vasus I am fire [Agni], and of the mountains I am Meru.

Of priests, O Arjuna, know Me to be the chief, Bṛhaspati, the lord of devotion. Of generals I am Skanda, the lord of war; and of bodies of water I am the ocean.

Of the great sages I am Bhṛgu; of vibrations I am the transcendental om. Of sacrifices I am the chanting of the holy names [japa], and of immovable things I am the Himalayas.

Of all trees I am the holy fig tree, and amongst sages and demigods I am Nārada. Of the singers of the gods [Gandharvas] I am Citraratha, and among perfected beings I am the sage Kapila.

Of horses know Me to be Uccaiḥśravā, who rose out of the ocean, born of the elixir of immortality; of lordly elephants I am Airāvata, and among men I am the monarch.

Of weapons I am the thunderbolt; among cows I am the surabhi, givers of abundant milk. Of procreators I am Kandarpa, the god of love, and of serpents I am Vāsuki, the chief.

Of the celestial Nāga snakes I am Ananta; of the aquatic deities I am Varuṇa. Of departed ancestors I am Aryamā, and among the dispensers of law I am Yama, lord of death.

Among the Daitya demons I am the devoted Prahlāda; among subduers I am time; among the beasts I am the lion, and among birds I am Garuḍa, the feathered carrier of Viṣṇu.

Of purifiers I am the wind; of the wielders of weapons I am Rāma; of fishes I am the shark, and of flowing rivers I am the Ganges.

Of all creations I am the beginning and the end and also the middle, O Arjuna. Of all sciences I am the spiritual science of the Self, and among logicians I am the conclusive truth.

Of letters I am the letter A, and among compounds I am the dual word. I am also inexhaustible time, and of creators I am Brahmā, whose manifold faces turn everywhere.

I am all-devouring death, and I am the generator of all things yet to be. Among women I am fame, fortune, speech, memory, intelligence, faithfulness and patience.

Of hymns I am the Bṛhat-sāma sung to the Lord Indra, and of poetry I am the Gāyatrī verse, sung daily by brāhmaṇas. Of months I am November and December, and of seasons I am flower-bearing spring.

I am also the gambling of cheats,[*] and of the splendid I am the splendour. I am victory, I am adventure, and I am the strength of the strong.

Of the descendants of Vṛṣni I am Vāsudeva, and of the Pāṇḍavas I am Arjuna. Of the sages I am Vyāsa, and among great thinkers I am Uśanā.

* Gambling is here representative of the ultimate form of cheating or deceit in the sense of deliberate calculation. The meaning is not to infer immorality to Krishna but to indicate metaphorically that Krishna cannot be outwitted and that He is in control of the destiny of the fraudulent.

Among punishments I am the rod of chastisement, and of those who seek victory, I am mortality. Of secret things I am silence, and of the wise I am wisdom.

Furthermore, O Arjuna, I am the generating seed of all existences. There is no being – moving or unmoving – that can exist without Me.

O mighty conqueror of enemies, there is no end to My divine manifestations. What I have spoken to you is but a mere indication of My infinite opulences.

Know that all beautiful, glorious, and mighty creations spring from but a spark of My splendour.

But what need is there, Arjuna, for all this detailed knowledge? With a single fragment of Myself I pervade and support this entire universe.

JUDAISM

———

Judaism is the oldest of the West's major living Faiths. It is the root from which Christianity, Islam and the Bahá'í Faith have sprung. This Faith does not originate with the great Prophet and Law-giver Moses but, rather, is rooted in a relationship with God that is said to have begun with the beginning of humankind's creation. Nevertheless, the record of its own sacred texts, the

Hebrew Scriptures, attribute the authorship of the first five books (the Pentateuch) to Moses.* These books present a history of human relations with God beginning with creation itself. Some view this record as a literal history of the world, others interpret it symbolically as eternal history in relation to the human soul.

Later apocryphal texts tell us that this original record was lost during a period when the Hebrew people had been forced into captivity in the ancient kingdom of Babylon.§ Eventually they were granted permission to return to Jerusalem and there, through the guidance of Ezra, the Law was restored to the lives of the people. These events are believed to have occurred sometime in the fifth century BC. Some scholars therefore date our version of these Scriptures from this period. Whatever period they were written in, their origin is very ancient, and their impact on civilization has been very great.

One of the most influential aspects of these ancient Scriptures is the Law which, according to the texts, was revealed by God to Moses on Mount Sinai. It is the revelation of this Law that has been selected for this section of *Accents of God*. Even most non-religious people in western countries are familiar with some abbreviated form of the Ten Commandments, but few have probably read them in their traditional, unedited form and in their Scriptural context.

The setting of the Ten Commandments or 'the Decalogue' - chapters nineteen and twenty of the Book of Exodus - is Mount Sinai in the Sinai Desert. Here, the Hebrew people have arrived

* Exodus 24:4-8, 34:27-8.

§ 2 Esdras 14:21-2.

after being freed from their long captivity in the land of Egypt and are camped at the base of the mountain. Moses is their deliverer who led them out of bondage, a Prophet raised up and assisted by God. The texts express the events of this deliverance in the form of miraculous happenings intended to convey the evidences and reality of divine sovereignty inherent in the Law.

Moses, however, is not only a deliverer in the sense of bringing His people physically out of the actual land of Egypt and away from the oppression of the Egyptian Pharaoh. More importantly, the giving of the Law is, in itself, a deliverance from the Egypt of self. An eternal theme of religion is evident here. Every soul is, in a sense, in bondage, here symbolized by the captivity of the Jews in Egypt. The Law is given as the means for attaining deliverance from this spiritual captivity. The first five* laws pertain to our relation to and understanding of the divine reality, God. The last five laws express the essential code of conduct that preserves the spiritual relationship between human beings. Together these laws provide the means for living a sanctified life acceptable to God and which preserves the happiness of humankind.

---

* The fifth command may at first appear otherwise in as much as it concerns respect for parents, but it relates specifically to the understanding and worship of God in that parents were the first instructors of children in the Law. The fifth command therefore preserves the primary hierarchy for the continuance of the religion.

✤

IN THE THIRD MONTH, when the children of Israel were
gone forth out of the land of Egypt, the same day came they into
the wilderness of Sinai. For they were departed from Rephidim,
and were come to the desert of Sinai, and had pitched in the
wilderness; and there Israel camped before the mount.

And Moses went up unto God, and the LORD called unto
him out of the mountain, saying, 'Thus shalt thou say to the house
of Jacob, and tell the children of Israel: "Ye have seen what I did
unto the Egyptians, and how I bare you on eagles' wings, and
brought you unto Myself. Now therefore, if ye will obey My
voice indeed, and keep My covenant, then ye shall be a peculiar
treasure unto Me above all people: for all the earth is Mine: And
ye shall be unto Me a kingdom of priests, and an holy nation."
These are the words which thou shalt speak unto the children of
Israel.'

And Moses came and called for the elders of the people, and
laid before their faces all these words which the LORD commanded
Him. And all the people answered together, and said, 'All that the
LORD hath spoken we will do'. And Moses returned the words of
the people unto the LORD. And the LORD said unto Moses, 'Lo, I
come unto thee in a thick cloud, that the people may hear when I
speak with thee, and believe thee forever'. And Moses told the

words of the people unto the LORD. And the LORD said unto Moses, 'Go unto the people, and sanctify them to day and to morrow, and let them wash their clothes, And be ready against the third day: for the third day the LORD will come down in the sight of all the people upon mount Sinai. And thou shalt set bounds unto the people round about, saying, "Take heed to yourselves, that ye go not up into the mount, or touch the border of it: whosoever toucheth the mount shall be surely put to death: There shall not an hand touch it, but he shall surely be stoned, or shot through; whether it be beast or man, it shall not live": when the trumpet soundeth long, they shall come up to the mount.'

And Moses went down from the mount unto the people, and sanctified the people; and they washed their clothes. And He said unto the people, 'Be ready against the third day: come not at your wives.' And it came to pass on the third day in the morning, that there were thunders and lightnings, and a thick cloud upon the mount, and the voice of the trumpet exceeding loud; so that all the people that were in the camp trembled.

And Moses brought forth the people out of the camp to meet with God; and they stood at the nether part of the mount. And mount Sinai was altogether on a smoke, because the LORD descended upon it in fire: and the smoke thereof ascended as the smoke of a furnace, and the whole mount quaked greatly. And when the voice of the trumpet sounded long, and waxed louder and louder, Moses spake, and God answered him by a voice. And the LORD came down upon mount Sinai, on the top of the mount: and the LORD called Moses up to the top of the mount; and Moses went up. And the LORD said unto Moses, 'Go down, charge the people, lest they break through unto the LORD to gaze, and many of them perish. And let the priests also, which come near to the LORD, sanctify themselves, lest the LORD break forth upon them.'

And Moses said unto the LORD, 'The people cannot come up to mount Sinai: for thou chargedst us, saying, "Set bounds about the mount, and sanctify it."' And the LORD said unto Him, 'Away, get thee down, and thou shalt come up, thou, and Aaron with thee: but let not the priests and the people break through to come up unto the LORD, lest He break forth upon them.' So Moses went down unto the people, and spake unto them.

And God spake all these words, saying, 'I am the LORD thy God, which have brought thee out of the land of Egypt, out of the house of bondage. Thou shalt have no other gods before me. Thou shalt not make unto thee any graven image, or any likeness of any thing that is in heaven above, or that is in the earth beneath, or that is in the water under the earth: Thou shalt not bow down thyself to them, nor serve them: for I the LORD thy God am a jealous God, visiting the iniquity of the fathers upon the children unto the third and fourth generation of them that hate me; And shewing mercy unto thousands of them that love me, and keep my commandments. Thou shalt not take the name of the LORD thy God in vain; for the LORD will not hold him guiltless that taketh his name in vain.

Remember the sabbath day, to keep it holy. Six days shalt thou labour, and do all thy work: But the seventh day is the sabbath of the LORD thy God: in it thou shalt not do any work, thou, nor thy son, nor thy daughter, thy manservant, nor thy maidservant, nor thy cattle, nor thy stranger that is within thy gates: For in six days the LORD made heaven and earth, the sea, and all that in them is, and rested the seventh day: wherefore the LORD blessed the sabbath day, and hallowed it.

Honour thy father and thy mother: that thy days may be long upon the land which the LORD thy God giveth thee. Thou shalt not kill. Thou shalt not commit adultery. Thou shalt not steal. Thou shalt not bear false witness against thy neighbour. Thou shalt not covet thy neighbour's house, thou shalt not covet thy neighbour's wife, nor his manservant, nor his maidservant, nor his ox, nor his ass, nor any thing that is thy neighbour's.'

And all the people saw the thunderings, and the lightnings, and the noise of the trumpet, and the mountain smoking: and when the people saw it, they removed, and stood afar off. And they said unto Moses, 'Speak thou with us, and we will hear: but let not God speak with us, lest we die.' And Moses said unto the people, 'Fear not: for God is come to prove you, and that his fear may be before your faces, that ye sin not.' And the people stood afar off, and Moses drew near unto the thick darkness where God was.

And the LORD said unto Moses, 'Thus thou shalt say unto the children of Israel, "Ye have seen that I have talked with you from heaven. Ye shall not make with Me gods of silver, neither shall ye make unto you gods of gold. An altar of earth thou shalt make unto Me, and shalt sacrifice thereon thy burnt offerings, and thy peace offerings, thy sheep, and thine oxen: in all places where I record my name I will come unto thee, and I will bless thee." '

BUDDHISM

⸺

Buddhism has its origin in North-East India, known today as Bihar. It was founded by Siddhartha Gautama, who is known by many titles but most commonly as the Buddha, meaning 'the fully enlightened one'. He is believed to have lived around 600 or 400 BC.

According to traditional belief, Siddhartha Gautama was born into royalty and lived a life of comfort but, upon venturing out into the wider world, He saw that human existence was afflicted by many forms of suffering. Overwhelmed with compassion for the human condition, He renounced His royalty and dedicated His life to remedying human suffering. The spiritual solution is said to have come to Him while meditating under a fig tree.

This account is usually taken as literal history. How much of it is actually historical is uncertain. The earliest accounts are not objective but are embellished with many symbols conveying the spiritual and divine nature of the Buddha and His awakening. In fact, the entire account easily lends itself to metaphorical interpretation. Buddha's royalty can signify the eternal world which exists outside the suffering of material existence. This was the world that the reality of Buddha inhabited, but in His love for humankind He 'descends', so to speak, from heaven and enters into the temporal world, taking on its mortal limitations and so suffering even as we do. He willingly does this in order to show us how to transcend life's sufferings and, in this way, impart to us a path to deliverance. Buddha shows that these limitations do not have to prevent us from attaining the imperishable and divine reality, known in Buddhism as Nirvana. He set forth these truths through both His teachings and His own example.

For this section of *Accents of God*, the Buddha's First Sermon has been chosen. This Sermon delineates the basic principles which constitute His remedy for human suffering and the path to enlightenment. The Sermon is also known as 'The Foundation of the Kingdom of Righteousness', or 'The Setting in Motion of the Wheel of Righteousness'. Hence Buddhism is commonly symbolized by a wheel with eight spokes, representing the eight different principles constituting the correct way of life.

The setting of the Sermon is Sarnath, at a place known as the deer park, located not far from present-day Varanasi. There it is said that Buddha delivered His First Sermon to five Bhikkus, that is, ascetics or mendicants. Previously, they had refused to believe that the Buddha knew the path to enlightenment and had little respect for Him because He did not follow a life of austerity as they did. One account records that only one of the mendicants was converted on hearing His discourse. Later, however, many people were converted and Buddha gathered together a number of disciples who laboured to spread His message.

Buddha's teachings are very straightforward and are among the easiest to grasp, but the style in which they have been conveyed through the centuries is generally perceived by western readers as excessively repetitious and tedious. Few books, therefore, present Buddhist literature in an unedited form. However, this type of composition, which repeats the preceding verses with only minor variations, may have developed to assist memorization and concentration and, thus, the preservation of the Buddha's message. How successful it was in accomplishing these goals is hard to ascertain, since any written record of events dating back over two thousand years and predating existing records by over five hundred years is bound to be problematic and difficult to authenticate.

Buddhism, like most religious traditions, has been interpreted in a variety of ways and has many different schools of thought. Some are decidedly non-theistic. This has prompted the oft-repeated question: 'Is Buddhism a religion or simply a philosophy?' Although there is an absence of teaching in existing canonical literature concerning a supreme God, Buddhism nevertheless possesses many characteristics that are distinctly religious. In the earliest Scriptures, for example, Buddha is clearly represented as the embodiment of the divine and eternal reality. Devotion to Him, reverence for His teachings, observance of the sacrificial life He prescribed, all suggest and typify what is commonly regarded as religious experience. Moreover, some Buddhist schools of thought regard faith in the Buddha's name as essential and salvation as a bestowal of His grace,* as certain branches of Christianity regard faith in Christ. Recent scholarship has also argued that early Buddhist texts are replete with indications that it was to be accepted as a divine revelation.§

The exact nature of Buddhism is a subject that may never be resolved in academic circles, but the basic truths of the Buddha's First Sermon are as evident and practicable today as they would be in any past or future age. They are eternal precepts which, although not expounding directly on the eternal (i.e., God), nevertheless provide the path for its attainment.

* See Kennith W. Morgan, *The Path of the Buddha* 336.
§ See Peter Masefield, *Divine Revelation in Pali Scripture*.

✹

Reverence to the Blessed One,
the Holy One, the Fully-Enlightened One.

THUS HAVE I HEARD. The Blessed One was once staying at
Benares, at the hermitage called Migadâya. And there the Blessed
One addressed the company of the five Bhikkhus, and said:

'There are two extremes, O Bhikkhus, which the man who
has given up the world ought not to follow - the habitual practice,
on the one hand, of those things whose attraction depends upon
the passions, and especially of sensuality - a low and pagan way (of
seeking satisfaction) unworthy, unprofitable, and fit only for the
worldly-minded - and the habitual practice, on the other hand, of
asceticism (or self-mortification), which is painful, unworthy, and
unprofitable.

'There is a middle path, O Bhikkhus, avoiding these two
extremes, discovered by the Tathâgata* - a path which opens the
eyes, and bestows understanding, which leads to peace of mind, to
the higher wisdom, to full enlightenment, to Nirvâna!§

* The Tathâgata is an epithet of the Buddha meaning one who has rightly
followed the path.
§ Signifies enlightenment, the cessation of selfish desires, and represents a state in
which the individual becomes free from the suffering and bonds of material
existence.

'What is that middle path, O Bhikkhus, avoiding these two extremes, discovered by the Tathâgata – that path which opens the eyes, and bestows understanding, which leads to peace of mind, to the higher wisdom, to full enlightenment, to Nirvâna? Verily! it is this noble eightfold path; that is to say:

> 'Right views;
>
> Right aspirations;
>
> Right speech;
>
> Right conduct;
>
> Right livelihood;
>
> Right effort;
>
> Right mindfulness; and
>
> Right contemplation.

'This, O Bhikkhus, is that middle path, avoiding these two extremes, discovered by the Tathâgata – that path which opens the eyes, and bestows understanding, which leads to peace of mind, to the higher wisdom, to full enlightenment, to Nirvâna!

'Now this, O Bhikkhus, is the noble truth concerning suffering. Birth is attended with pain, decay is painful, disease is painful, death is painful. Union with the unpleasant is painful, painful is separation from the pleasant; and any craving that is unsatisfied, that too is painful. In brief, the five aggregates which spring from attachment (the conditions of individuality and their cause)are painful. This then, O Bhikkhus, is the noble truth concerning suffering.

'Now this, O Bhikkhus, is the noble truth concerning the origin of suffering. Verily, it is that thirst (or craving), causing the renewal of existence, accompanied by sensual delight, seeking satisfaction now here, now there - that is to say, the craving for the gratification of the passions, or the craving for (a future) life, or the craving for success (in this present life). This then, O Bhikkhus, is the noble truth concerning the origin of suffering.

'Now this, O Bhikkhus, is the noble truth concerning the destruction of suffering. Verily, it is the destruction, in which no passion remains, of this very thirst; the laying aside of, the getting rid of, the being free from, the harbouring no longer of this thirst. This then, O Bhikkhus, is the noble truth concerning the destruction of suffering.

'Now this, O Bhikkhus, is the noble truth concerning the way which leads to the destruction of sorrow. Verily! it is this noble eightfold path; that is to say:

'Right views;
Right aspirations;
Right speech;
Right conduct;
Right livelihood;
Right effort;
Right mindfulness; and
Right contemplation.

'This then, O Bhikkhus, is the noble truth concerning the destruction of sorrow.

'That this was the noble truth concerning sorrow, was not, O Bhikkhus, among the doctrines handed down, but there arose within me the eye (to perceive it), there arose the knowledge (of its nature), there arose the understanding (of its cause), there arose the wisdom (to guide in the path of tranquillity), there arose the light (to dispel darkness from it).

'And again, O Bhikkhus, that I should comprehend that this was the noble truth concerning sorrow, though it was not among the doctrines handed down, there arose within me the eye, there arose the knowledge, there arose the understanding, there arose the wisdom, there arose the light.

'And again, O Bhikkhus, that I had comprehended that this was the noble truth concerning sorrow, though it was not among the doctrines handed down, there arose within me the eye, there arose the knowledge, there arose the understanding, there arose the wisdom, there arose the light.

'That this was the noble truth concerning the origin of sorrow, though it was not among the doctrines handed down, there arose within me the eye; but there arose within me the knowledge, there arose the understanding, there arose the wisdom, there arose the light

'And again, O Bhikkhus, that I should put away the origin of sorrow, though the noble truth concerning it was not among the doctrines handed down, there arose within me the eye, there arose the knowledge, there arose the understanding, there arose the wisdom, there arose the light.

'And again, O Bhikkhus, that I had fully put away the origin of sorrow, though the noble truth concerning it was not among the doctrines handed down, there arose within me the eye, there arose the knowledge, there arose the understanding, there arose the wisdom, there arose the light.

'That this, O Bhikkhus, was the noble truth concerning the destruction of sorrow, though it was not among the doctrines handed down; but there arose within me the eye, there arose the knowledge, there arose the understanding, there arose the wisdom, there arose the light

'And again, O Bhikkhus, that I should fully realise the destruction of sorrow, though the noble truth concerning it was not among the doctrines handed down, there arose within me the eye, there arose the knowledge, there arose the understanding, there arose the wisdom, there arose the light.

'And again, O Bhikkhus, that I had fully realised the destruction of sorrow, though the noble truth concerning it was not among the doctrines handed down, there arose within me the eye, there arose the knowledge, there arose the understanding, there arose the wisdom, there arose the light.

'That this was the noble truth concerning the way which leads to the destruction of sorrow, was not, O Bhikkhus, among the doctrines handed down; but there arose within me the eye, there arose the knowledge, there arose the understanding, there arose the wisdom, there arose the light.

'And again, O Bhikkhus, that I should become versed in the way which leads to the destruction of sorrow, though the noble truth concerning it was not among the doctrines handed down, there arose within me the eye, there arose the knowledge, there arose the understanding, there arose the wisdom, there arose the light.

'And again, O Bhikkhus, that I had become versed in the way which leads to the destruction of sorrow, though the noble truth concerning it was not among the doctrines handed down, there arose within me the eye, there arose the knowledge, there arose the understanding, there arose the wisdom, there arose the light.

'So long, O Bhikkhus, as my knowledge and insight were not quite clear, regarding each of these four noble truths in this triple order, in this twelvefold manner - so long was I uncertain whether I had attained to the full insight of that wisdom which is unsurpassed in the heavens or on earth, among the whole race of Samanas and Brâhmans, or of gods or men.

'But as soon, O Bhikkhus, as my knowledge and insight were quite clear regarding each of these four noble truths, in this triple order, in this twelvefold manner - then did I become certain that I had attained to the full insight of that wisdom which is unsurpassed in the heavens or on earth, among the whole race of Samanas and Brâhmans, or of gods or men.   And now this knowledge and this insight has arisen within me.   Immovable is the emancipation of my heart.   This is my last existence.   There will now be no rebirth for me!'

Thus spake the Blessed One. The company of the five Bhikkhus, glad at heart, exalted the words of the Blessed One. And when the discourse had been uttered, there arose within the venerable Kondañña* the eye of truth, spotless, and without a stain, (and he saw that) whatsoever has an origin, in that is also inherent the necessity of coming to an end.

---

* Kondañña is one of the five Bhikkhus or mendicants to whom the Buddha addressed His Sermon.

And when the royal chariot wheel of the truth had thus been set rolling onwards by the Blessed One, the gods of the earth gave forth a shout, saying: 'In Benares, at the hermitage of the Migadâya, the supreme wheel of the empire of Truth has been set rolling by the Blessed One - that wheel which not by any Samana or Brâhman*, not by any god, not by any Brahma§ or Mâra**, not by any one in the universe, can ever be turned back!'

And when they heard the shout of the gods of the earth, the attendant gods of the four great kings (the guardian angels of the four quarters of the globe) gave forth a shout, saying: 'In Benares, at the hermitage of the Migadâya, the supreme wheel of the empire of Truth has been set rolling by the Blessed One - that wheel which not by any Samana or Brâhman, not by any god, not by any Brahma or Mâra, not by any one in the universe, can ever be turned back!'

[And thus as the gods in each of the heavens heard the shout of the inhabitants of the heaven beneath, they took up the cry until the gods in the highest heaven of heavens] gave forth the shout, saying: 'In Benares, at the hermitage of the Migadâya, the supreme wheel of the empire of Truth has been set rolling by the Blessed

---

* Brâhman is a term used to refer to the highest caste, or class, in the Hindu social structure; it also signifies the Supreme Being. In this context it indicates that no scholar or priest has put forth teachings such as the Buddha, and in this way Buddha delineates the special, divine nature of His message even as Prophets in the Western religious tradition set forth the claim to divine Revelation.

§ The use of the word *Brahma* here appears to signify that no supreme reality will turn back the truth of Buddha's teachings in as much as it would constitute a contradiction in terms of divine reality. Buddha appears to be asserting the eternal and divine nature of His teachings.

** The personification of evil.

One - that wheel which not by any Sama*n*a or Brâhman, not by any god, not by any Brahma or Mâra, not by any one in the universe, can ever be turned back!'

And thus, in an instant, a second, a moment, the sound went up even to the world of Brahma: and this great ten-thousand-world-system quaked and trembled and was shaken violently*, and an immeasurable bright light appeared in the universe, beyond even the power of the gods!

Then did the Blessed One give utterance to this exclamation of joy: 'Konda*ññ*a hath realised it. Konda*ññ*a hath realised it!' And so the venerable Konda*ññ*a acquired the name of A*ññ*âta§-Konda*ññ*a ('the Konda*ññ*a who realised').

---

* Religious orders, while originally divinely inspired, go into decline after a long period of time and become ineffective and corrupted by self-seeking individuals. It is very probable that the violent shaking described here symbolizes the impact of the Buddha's teachings on the established religious order which Buddha sought to displace institutionally and purify spiritually. A similar use of the same symbolism is employed to convey the impact of the crucifixion of Christ on the institutions of Judaism (Matthew 27:50-1).

§ A*ññ*âtta means substanceless and here signifies transcendence on the part of Konda*ññ*a who has recognized the truth of Buddha's teachings.

CHRISTIANITY

Of the world's great religions today, Christianity has spread the farthest and gathered the most adherents, if we include all the sects that have evolved over the centuries since its inception. As with all the religions discussed in this book, Christianity does not claim to embody the first revelation from God. It recognizes the truth of a religious tradition that has preceded it and presents itself as a further outpouring of the divine grace which has existed in the world since the beginning of time.

Its founder, Jesus Christ, was born among the Jews of Palestine nearly two thousand years ago. The exact date of Jesus' birth is disputed, but it is believed that He was around thirty years old when He actively set out to fulfil His mission. His ministry was short and turbulent, lasting only three years.

He was born into a time characterized by religious crisis and expectation. The Jews among whom He lived had long awaited the Messiah whose advent was promised in their sacred Scriptures and who they expected to be a political and religious ruler. Their hope was that this Messiah would appear, throw off Roman domination and re-establish the kingdom that they once enjoyed in a former, more prosperous time. When Jesus began to preach, many thought that He might be the fulfilment of their expectations. However, when they realized that He had not come to lead armies against the Romans they quickly turned against Him.

He not only showed no interest in politics, He indicated that the Jews had misunderstood the implications of the sacred books of the Bible. He was, in fact, the Messiah, but the deliverance He brought was a deliverance from sin, and the kingdom He came to establish was the Kingdom of God within the heart of the believer. Despite the benevolence of His teachings He was opposed and His greatest opponents were the religious leaders of His day, the Pharisees and Scribes. To them Jesus was definitely not the Messiah, but a dangerous heretic whose popularity might provoke the anger of the Romans.

These religious leaders also regarded Him as a challenge to their own authority. Many of His teachings struck them as blasphemous. Jesus said that He had come down from heaven* and that He was the Son of God.§ Moreover, He pointed out the corruption of the Pharisees, calling them hypocrites and warning the people against them. Through His own example He taught that it was not the letter of the Law that mattered most but, rather, its spirit. To maintain this spirit, Jesus indicated that the older religious forms and practices needed to be abandoned.

For this section of *Accents of God*, Jesus' Sermon on the Mount has been chosen. This Sermon embodies Jesus' own teachings concerning the spirit of the Law, the right religious life and attainment to the Kingdom of God. It is the longest of Jesus' discourses and the epitome of His ethical teachings. It has been the subject of numerous interpretations and has inspired so many books and commentaries over the years that no one has yet attempted to catalogue them.

According to tradition the setting is a mount, now known as the Mountain of the Beatitudes**, overlooking the Sea of Galilee in present-day Israel.

* John, ch. 6.
§ John, ch. 10.
** Beatitudes refers to verses 3–11 of the Sermon.

❂

AND SEEING THE MULTITUDES, He went up into a mountain and when He was set, His disciples came unto Him: And He opened His mouth, and taught them, saying,

Blessed are the poor in spirit: for theirs is the kingdom of heaven.

Blessed are they that mourn: for they shall be comforted.

Blessed are the meek: for they shall inherit the earth.

Blessed are they which do hunger and thirst after righteousness: for they shall be filled.

Blessed are the merciful: for they shall obtain mercy.

Blessed are the pure in heart: for they shall see God.

Blessed are the peacemakers: for they shall be called the children of God.

Blessed are they which are persecuted for righteousness' sake: for theirs is the kingdom of heaven.

Blessed are ye, when men shall revile you, and persecute you, and shall say all manner of evil against you falsely, for my sake. Rejoice, and be exceeding glad: for great is your reward in heaven: for so persecuted they the prophets which were before you.

Ye are the salt of the earth: but if the salt have lost his savour, wherewith shall it be salted? it is thenceforth good for nothing, but to be cast out, and to be trodden under foot of men. Ye are the light of the world. A city that is set on an hill cannot be hid.

Neither do men light a candle, and put it under a bushel, but on a candlestick; and it giveth light unto all that are in the house. Let your light so shine before men, that they may see your good works, and glorify your Father which is in heaven.

Think not that I am come to destroy the law, or the prophets: I am not come to destroy, but to fulfil. For verily I say unto you, Till heaven and earth pass, one jot or one tittle shall in no wise pass from the law, till all be fulfiled. Whosoever therefore shall break one of these least commandments, and shall teach men so, he shall be called the least in the kingdom of heaven: but whosoever shall do and teach them, the same shall be called great in the kingdom of heaven. For I say unto you, That except your righteousness shall exceed the righteousness of the scribes and Pharisees,* ye shall in no case enter into the kingdom of heaven.

Ye have heard that it was said by them of old time, Thou shalt not kill; and whosoever shall kill shall be in danger of the judgment. But I say unto you, That whosoever is angry with his brother without a cause shall be in danger of the judgment and whosoever shall say to his brother, Raca,§ shall be in danger of the council. But whosoever shall say, Thou fool, shall be in danger of hell fire.

* Jewish priests of a particular religious party.
§ This is probably derived from Aramaic and means 'fool'. The message appears to be that it is not permissible to denigrate others out of resentment.

Therefore if thou bring thy gift to the altar, and there rememberest that thy brother hath ought against thee; Leave there thy gift before the altar and go thy way, first be reconciled to thy brother, and then come and offer thy gift. Agree with thine adversary quickly, whiles thou art in the way with him; lest at any time the adversary deliver thee to the judge, and the judge deliver thee to the officer, and thou be cast into prison. Verily I say unto thee, Thou shalt by no means come out thence, till thou hast paid the uttermost farthing.

Ye have heard that it was said by them of old time, Thou shalt not commit adultery. But I say unto you, That whosoever looketh on a woman to lust after her hath committed adultery with her already in his heart. And if thy right eye offend thee, pluck it out, and cast it from thee: for it is profitable for thee that one of thy members should perish, and not that thy whole body should be cast into hell. And if thy right hand offend thee, cut it off, and cast it from thee: for it is profitable for thee that one of thy members should perish, and not that thy whole body should be cast into hell.

It hath been said, Whosoever shall put away his wife, let him give her a writing of divorcement: But I say unto you, That whosoever shall put away his wife, saving for the cause of fornication, causeth her to commit adultery: and whosoever shall marry her that is divorced committeth adultery. Again, ye have heard that it hath been said by them of old time, Thou shalt not forswear thyself, but shalt perform unto the Lord thine oaths: But I say unto you, Swear not at all; neither by heaven; for it is God's throne: Nor by the earth, for it is His footstool: neither by

Jerusalem; for it is the city of the great King. Neither shalt thou swear by thy head, because thou canst not make one hair white or black. But let your communication be, Yea, yea; Nay, nay: for whatsoever is more than these cometh of evil. Ye have heard that it hath been said, An eye for an eye, and a tooth for a tooth: But I say unto you, That ye resist not evil: but whosoever shall smite thee on thy right cheek, turn to him the other also. And if any man will sue thee at the law, and take away thy coat, let him have thy cloak also. And whosoever shall compel thee to go a mile, go with him twain. Give to him that asketh thee, and from him that would borrow of thee turn not thou away. Ye have heard that it hath been said, Thou shalt love thy neighbour, and hate thine enemy. But I say unto you, Love your enemies, bless them that curse you, do good to them that hate you, and pray for them which despitefully use you, and persecute you; That ye may be the children of your Father which is in heaven: for He maketh His sun to rise on the evil and on the good, and sendeth rain on the just and on the unjust.

For if ye love them which love you, what reward have ye? do not even the publicans the same? And if ye salute your brethren only, what do ye more than others? do not even the publicans so? Be ye therefore perfect, even as your Father which is in heaven is perfect.

Take heed that ye do not your alms before men, to be seen of them: otherwise ye have no reward of your Father which is in heaven. Therefore when thou doest thine alms, do not sound a trumpet before thee, as the hypocrites do in the synagogues and in the streets, that they may have glory of men. Verily I say unto they have their reward. But when thou doest alms, let not thy left hand know what thy right hand doeth that thine alms may be in secret and thy Father which seeth in secret himself shall reward thee openly. And when thou prayest, thou shalt not be as the hypocrites are: for they love to pray standing in the synagogues and in the corners of the streets, that they may be seen of men. Verily I say unto you, they have their reward. But thou, when thou prayest, enter into thy closet, and when thou hast shut thy door, pray to thy Father which is in secret; and thy Father which seeth in secret shall reward thee openly. But when ye pray, use not vain repetitions, as the heathen do, for they think that they shall be heard for their much speaking. Be not ye therefore like unto them: for your Father knoweth what things ye have need of before ye ask him. After this manner therefore pray ye:

> Our Father which art in heaven, Hallowed be thy name. Thy kingdom come. Thy will be done in earth, as it is in heaven. Give us this day our daily bread. And forgive us our debts, as we forgive our debtors. And lead us not into temptation, but deliver us from evil: For thine is the kingdom, and the power, and the glory, for ever. Amen.*

For if ye forgive men their trespasses, your heavenly Father will also forgive you: But if ye forgive not men their trespasses, neither will your Father forgive your trespasses.

---

* *'Amen'*, a Hebrew word meaning 'surely', here signifying firm acceptance of what has been said.

Moreover when ye fast, be not, as the hypocrites, of a sad countenance: for they disfigure their faces, that they may appear unto men to fast. Verily I say unto you, they have their reward. But thou, when thou fastest, anoint thine head, and wash thy face; That thou appear not unto men to fast, but unto thy Father which is in secret: and thy Father, which seeth in secret, shall reward thee openly.

Lay not up for yourselves treasures upon earth, where moth and rust doth corrupt, and where thieves break through and steal: But lay up for yourselves treasures in heaven, where neither moth nor rust doth corrupt, and where thieves do not break through nor steal: For where your treasure is, there will your heart be also.

The light of the body is the eye, if therefore thine eye be single, thy whole body shall be full of light. But if thine eye be evil, thy whole body shall be full of darkness. If therefore the light that is in thee be darkness, how great is that darkness!

No man can serve two masters: for either he will hate the one, and love the other; or else he will hold to the one, and despise the other. Ye cannot serve God and mammon. Therefore I say unto you, Take no thought for your life, what ye shall eat, or what ye shall drink; nor yet for your body, what ye shall put on. Is not the life more than meat, and the body than raiment? Behold the fowls of the air, for they sow not, neither do they reap, nor gather into barns; yet your heavenly Father feedeth them. Are ye not much better than they?

Which of you by taking thought can add one cubit unto his stature? And why take ye thought for raiment? Consider the lilies of the field, how they grow; they toil not, neither do they spin.

And yet I say unto you, that even Solomon in all his glory was not arrayed like one of these. Wherefore, if God so clothe the grass of the field, which today is, and tomorrow is cast into the oven, shall he not much more clothe you, O ye of little faith?

Therefore take no thought, saying, What shall we eat? or, What shall we drink? or, Wherewithal shall we be clothed? (For after all these things do the Gentiles seek:) for your heavenly Father knoweth that ye have need of all these things. But seek ye first the kingdom of God, and His righteousness; and all these things shall be added unto you. Take therefore no thought for the morrow: for the morrow shall take thought for the things of itself. Sufficient unto the day is the evil thereof.

Judge not, that ye be not judged. For with what judgment ye judge, ye shall be judged: and with what measure ye mete, it shall be measured to you again. And why beholdest thou the mote that is in thy brother's eye, but considerest not the beam that is in thine own eye? Or how wilt thou say to thy brother, Let me pull out the mote out of thine eye; and, behold, a beam is in thine own eye?

Thou hypocrite, first cast out the beam out of thine own eye; and then shalt thou see clearly to cast out the mote out of thy brother's eye. Give not that which is holy unto the dogs, neither cast ye your pearls before swine, lest they trample them under their feet, and turn again and rend you. Ask, and it shall be given you; seek, and ye shall find; knock, and it shall be opened unto you: For every one that asketh receiveth; and he that seeketh findeth; and to him that knocketh it shall be opened. Or what man is there of you, whom if his son ask bread, will he give him a stone? Or if he

ask a fish, will he give him a serpent? If ye then, being evil, know
how to give good gifts unto your children, how much more shall
your Father which is in heaven give good things to them that ask
him?

Therefore all things whatsoever ye would that men should do
to you, do ye even so to them: for this is the law and the prophets.
Enter ye in at the strait gate: for wide is the gate, and broad is the
way, that leadeth to destruction, and many there be which go in
thereat: Because strait is the gate, and narrow is the way, which
leadeth unto life, and few there be that find it.

Beware of false prophets, which come to you in sheep's
clothing, but inwardly they are ravening wolves. Ye shall know
them by their fruits. Do men gather grapes of thorns, or figs of
thistles? Even so every good tree bringeth forth good fruit; but a
corrupt tree bringeth forth evil fruit. A good tree cannot bring
forth evil fruit, neither can a corrupt tree bring forth good fruit.
Every tree that bringeth not forth good fruit is hewn down, and
cast into the fire. Wherefore by their fruits ye shall know them.
Not every one that saith unto me, Lord, Lord, shall enter into the
kingdom of heaven; but he that doeth the will of my Father which
is in heaven.

Many will say to me in that day, Lord, Lord, have we not
prophesied in thy name? and in thy name have cast out devils? and
in thy name done many wonderful works? And then will I profess
unto them, I never knew you: depart from me, ye that work
iniquity. Therefore whosoever heareth these sayings of mine, and
doeth them, I will liken him unto a wise man, which built his
house upon a rock: And the rain descended, and the floods came,

and the winds blew, and beat upon that house; and it fell not: or it was founded upon a rock. And every one that heareth these sayings of mine, and doeth them not, shall be likened unto a foolish man, which built his house upon the sand: And the rain descended, and the floods came, and the winds blew, and beat upon that house; and it fell: and great was the fall of it.

And it came to pass, when Jesus had ended these sayings, the people were astonished at His doctrine: For He taught them as one having authority, and not as the scribes. When He was come down from the mountain, great multitudes followed Him.

ISLAM

The religion of Islam, which means 'submission', or more specifically submission to the will of God, is based on the teachings of the Qur'án. The Qur'án is regarded by Muslims as the direct teachings of God, or the Word of God, revealed through the Prophet Muḥammad. In setting forth the Faith of Islam, Muslims believe that Muḥammad brought about a restoration of the true Faith of God established by Abraham.

Muḥammad was born during the latter part of the sixth century and was around forty years old in AD 610 when He first took up His prophetic mission. As a Prophet He was called upon to perform the difficult task of reforming the then extremely barbarous and polytheistic culture of His native Arabia. To achieve this He had to overcome violent opposition from the wealthier and more powerful social forces of His time. These difficulties and cultural conditions are, no doubt, responsible in part for the form of expression the Qur'án takes. Drawing upon the biblical stories that had penetrated the Arabian peninsula, He repeatedly reminded the people of the lessons found in the Bible.

In particular, He emphasized such instances as the flood in the days of Noah, the plagues visited on the Egyptians, the drowning of Pharaoh's armies and so forth. Through these stories He sought to strike fear into the hearts of His hearers and enemies and warn them of the consequences of turning against God and living an unjust life. On the other hand, when speaking about those who were faithful to God and who abided by spiritual precepts and laws, Muḥammad emphasized the mercy and compassion of God.

Throughout the Qur'án, the reader is confronted by the message of reward and punishment. Coupled with this message is the dominating theme of the majesty and power of God. The effect of these teachings is to inspire an approach to life that is completely God-centred. That is, all things are seen in relation to the will of one supreme and just God. In this way, a path is provided whereby the believer sees the divine reality at work in all aspects of his or her life.

For this section of *Accents of God*, the fortieth surah, or chapter, of the Qur'án has been chosen. This surah, called 'The Forgiving One' or 'The Believer', depending on the translation, has all the basic characteristics discussed above. The setting of its revelation is the city of Mecca located in a barren desert valley in the Arabian peninsula. In Muḥammad's day, Mecca was known as a favoured stop on an important trading route. It was also the site of a religious sanctuary housing a variety of images representing different gods.

With the eventual triumph of Islam in the region, Mecca came under Muḥammad's control. The sanctuary, known as the Ka'bah, was then cleansed of images and dedicated to the same God spoken of throughout the Bible, which Muḥammad taught was the only God, the God of all peoples*. The Ka'bah became the most important religious site of the Islamic religion and remains the main centre of pilgrimage for Muslims.

*In Arabic, God is referred to as '*Allah*'. This difference of language led some European critics to imagine that the God of Islam is another or different God from that of the Bible. Muḥammad, however, firmly identified His message with that of the Bible and affirmed that the God spoken of in Jewish and Christian Scripture is the same God of the Qur'án: 'We believe in the revelation which hath been sent down unto us, and also in that which hath been sent down unto you; our God and your God is one, and unto Him are we resigned' (Qur'án 29:45-46). Also, the Arabic '*Allah*' is rooted in the same Semitic speech as the Hebrew '*El*' and '*Elohim*'. The Arabic, '*ilah*' is the same as the Hebrew '*elah*', and '*Allah*' is believed to be arrived at by the addition of the definite article '*al*' (*Al-ilah*) to form '*Allah*', *the God*. The Hebrew Prophet Daniel, e.g., says, 'Blessed be the name of God [*elah*] forever' (Dan. 2:20). Here the Hebrew is essentially the same as Arabic, whereas, the English word '*God*' is derived from ancient European tribal religion and is not used in either the original Hebrew or Greek Bible.

The actual text of the Qur'án, some of which was written down during Muḥammad's life, was canonized during the lifetime of those who actually knew Muḥammad. These facts, plus the existence of very early editions, support its reliability.

✹

In the name of the Most Merciful God

THE REVELATION OF THIS BOOK is from the mighty, the wise GOD; the forgiver of sin, and the accepter of repentance; severe in punishing; long-suffering. There is no GOD but He: before Him shall be the general assembly at the last day. None disputeth against the signs of GOD, except the unbelievers: but let not their prosperous dealing in the land deceive thee with vain allurement.

The people of Noah, and the confederated infidels that were after them, accused their respective prophets of imposture before these; and each nation hatched ill designs against their apostle, that they might get him into their power; and they disputed with vain reasoning, that they might thereby invalidate the truth: wherefore I chastised them; and how severe was my punishment! Thus hath the sentence of thy LORD justly passed on the unbelievers; that they shall be the inhabitants of hell fire.

The angels who bear the throne of God, and those who stand about it, celebrate the praise of their LORD, and believe in Him; and they ask pardon for the true believers, saying, O LORD, thou encompassest all things by thy mercy and knowledge; wherefore forgive those who repent and follow thy path, and deliver them from the pains of hell: O LORD, lead them also into gardens of eternal abode, which thou hast promised unto them, and unto every one who shall do right, of their fathers, and their wives, and their children; for thou art the mighty, the wise GOD. And deliver them from evil; for whomsoever thou shalt deliver from evil on that day, on him wilt thou show mercy; and this will be great salvation.

But the infidels, at the day of judgement, shall hear a voice crying unto them, Verily the hatred of GOD towards you is more grievous than your hatred towards yourselves: since ye were called unto the faith, and would not believe. They shall say, O LORD, thou hast given us death twice, and thou hast twice given us life; and we confess our sins: is there therefore no way to get forth from this fire? And it shall be answered them, This hath befallen you, for that when one GOD was preached unto you, ye believed not; but if a plurality of gods had been associated with him, ye had believed; and judgement belongeth unto the high, the great GOD.

It is He who showeth you his signs, and sendeth down food unto you from heaven: but none will be admonished except he who turneth himself unto God. Call therefore upon GOD, exhibiting your religion pure unto him although the infidels be averse thereto. He is the Being of exalted degree, the possessor of the throne; who sendeth down the spirit, at His command, on such of His servants as He pleaseth; that He may warn mankind of the day of meeting, the day whereon they shall come forth out of their graves, and nothing of what concerneth them shall be hidden from GOD.

Unto whom will the kingdom belong on that day? Unto the only, the almighty GOD. On that day shall every soul be rewarded according to its merits; there shall be no injustice done on that day. Verily GOD will be swift in taking an account. Wherefore warn them, O Prophet, of the day which shall suddenly approach; when men's hearts shall come up to their throats, and strangle them. The ungodly shall have no friend or intercessor who shall be heard. GOD will know the deceitful eye, and that which their breasts conceal; and GOD will judge with truth: but the false gods which they invoke besides Him, shall not judge at all; for GOD is He who heareth and seeth.

Have they not gone through the earth and seen what hath been the end of those who were before them? They were more mighty than these in strength, and left more considerable footsteps of their power in the earth: yet GOD chastised them for their sins, and there was none to protect them from GOD. This they suffered, because their apostles had come unto them with evident signs, and they disbelieved: wherefore GOD chastised them; for he is strong, and severe in punishing.

We heretofore sent Moses with our signs and manifest power, unto Pharaoh, and Haman, and Karûn and they said, He is a sorcerer and a liar. And when he came unto them with the truth from us, they said, Slay the sons of those who have believed with him, and save their daughters alive; but the stratagem of the infidels was no other than vain.

And Pharaoh said, Let me alone, that I may kill Moses; and let Him call upon His LORD: verily I fear lest He change your religion, or cause violence to appear in the earth. And Moses said unto His people, Verily I have recourse unto my LORD, and your LORD, to defend Me against every proud person, who believeth not in the day of account. And a man who was a true believer, of the family of Pharaoh, and concealed his faith, said, Will ye put a man to death, because he saith, GOD is my LORD; seeing, he is come unto you with evident signs from your LORD? If he be a liar, on him will the punishment of his falsehood light; but if he speaketh the truth, some of those judgements with which he threateneth you, will fall upon you: verily GOD directeth not him who is a transgressor or a liar.

O my people, the kingdom is yours this day; and ye are conspicuous in the earth: but who shall defend us from the scourge of GOD, if it come unto us? Pharaoh said, I only propose to you what I think to be most expedient: and I guide you only into the right path. And he who had believed, said, O my people, verily I fear for you a day like that of the confederates against the Prophets in former times; a condition like that of the people of Noah, and the tribes of 'Ad, and T̲hámud and of those who have lived after them: for GOD willeth not that any injustice be done unto his servants. O my people, verily I fear for you the day whereon men shall call unto one another; the day whereon ye shall be turned back from the tribunal, and driven to hell: then shall ye have none to protect you against GOD.

And he whom GOD shall cause to err, shall have no director. Joseph came unto you, before Moses, with evident signs; but ye ceased not to doubt of the religion which he preached unto you, until, when he died, ye said, GOD will by no means send another apostle, after him. Thus doth GOD cause him to err, who is a transgressor and a sceptic. They who dispute against the signs of GOD, without any authority which hath come unto them, are in great abomination with GOD, and with those who believe. Thus doth GOD seal up every proud and stubborn heart.

And Pharaoh said, O Haman, build me a tower, that I may reach the tracts, the tracts of heaven, and may view the GOD of Moses; for I verily think him to be a liar. And thus the evil of his work was prepared for Pharaoh, and he turned aside from the right path: and the stratagems of Pharaoh ended only in loss. And he who had believed, said, O my people, follow me: I will guide you into the right way.

O my people, verily this present life is but a temporary enjoyment; but the life to come is the mansion of firm continuance. Whoever worketh evil, shall only be rewarded in equal proportion to the same: but whoever worketh good, whether male or female, and is a true believer, they shall enter paradise; they shall be provided for therein superabundantly.

And, O my people, as for me, I invite you to salvation; but ye invite me to hell fire: ye invite me to deny GOD, and to associate with him that whereof I have no knowledge; but I invite you to the most mighty, the forgiver of sins. There is no doubt but that the false gods to which ye invite me, deserve not to be invoked, either in this world or in the next; and that we must return unto GOD; and that the transgressors shall be the inhabitants of hell fire: and ye shall then remember what I now say unto you.

And I commit my affair unto GOD: for GOD regardeth his servants. Wherefore GOD delivered him from the evils which they had devised; and a grievous punishment encompassed the people of Pharaoh. They shall be exposed to the fire of hell morning and evening; and the day whereon the hour of judgement shall come, it shall be said unto them, Enter, O people of Pharaoh, into a most severe torment.

And think on the time when the infidels shall dispute together in hell fire; and the weak shall say unto those who behaved with arrogance, Verily we were your followers: will ye, therefore, relieve us from any part of this fire? Those who behaved with arrogance shall answer, Verily we are all doomed to suffer therein: for GOD hath now judged between His servants. And they who shall be in the fire, shall say unto the keepers of hell, Call ye on your LORD, that He would ease us, for one day, from this punishment. They shall answer, Did not your apostles come unto you with evident proofs? They shall say, Yea. The keepers shall reply, Do ye therefore call on God: but the calling of the unbelievers on Him shall be only in vain.

We will surely assist our apostles, and those who believe, in this present life, and on the day whereon the witnesses shall stand forth: a day, whereon the excuse of the unbelievers shall not avail them; but a curse shall attend them, and a wretched abode.

We heretofore gave unto Moses a direction: and we left as an inheritance unto the children of Israel the book of the Law; a direction, and an admonition to men of understanding. Wherefore do thou, O Prophet, bear the insults of the infidels with patience; for the promise of GOD is true: and ask pardon for thy fault; and celebrate the praise of thy LORD, in the evening and in the morning.

As to those who impugn the signs of GOD, without any convincing proof which hath been revealed unto them, there is nothing but pride in their breasts; but they shall not attain their desire: wherefore, fly for refuge unto GOD, for it is He who heareth and seeth.

Verily the creation of heaven and earth is more considerable than the creation of man: but the greater part of men do not understand. The blind and the seeing shall not be held equal; nor they who believe and work righteousness, and the evil-doer: how few revolve these things in their mind! The last hour will surely come; there is no doubt thereof: but the greater part of men believe it not. Your LORD saith, Call upon me, and I will hear you: but they who proudly disdain my service shall enter with ignominy into hell.

It is GOD who hath appointed the night for you to take your rest therein, and the day to give you light: verily GOD is endued with beneficence towards mankind; but the greater part of men do not give thanks. This is GOD, your LORD; the Creator of all things: there is no GOD besides him: how therefore are ye turned aside from his worship? Thus are they turned aside who oppose the signs of GOD.

It is GOD who hath given you the earth for a stable floor, and the heaven for a ceiling: and who hath formed you, and made your forms beautiful, and feedeth you with good things. This is GOD, your LORD. Wherefore, blessed be GOD, the LORD of all creatures! He is the living God: there is no GOD but He. Wherefore call upon Him, exhibiting unto Him the pure religion. Praise be unto GOD, the LORD of all creatures!

Say, Verily I am forbidden to worship the deities which ye invoke, besides GOD, after that evident proofs have come unto me from my LORD; and I am commanded to resign myself unto the LORD of all creatures. It is He who first created you of dust, and afterwards of seed, and afterwards of coagulated blood; and afterwards brought you forth infants out of your mothers' wombs: then He permitteth you to attain your age of full strength, and afterwards to grow old men (but some of you die before that age), and to arrive at the determined period of your life; that peradventure ye may understand. It is He who giveth life, and causeth to die: and when he decreeth a thing, He only saith unto it, Be, and it is.

Dost thou not observe those who dispute against the signs of GOD, how they are turned aside from the true faith? They who charge with falsehood the book of the Koran, and the other scriptures and revealed doctrines which we sent our former apostles to preach, shall hereafter know their folly; when the collars shall be on their necks, and the chains by which they shall be dragged into hell: then shall they be burned in the fire.

And it shall be said unto them, Where are the gods which ye associated beside GOD? They shall answer, They have withdrawn themselves from us: yea, we called on nothing heretofore. Thus doth GOD lead the unbelievers into error. This hath befallen you, for that ye rejoiced insolently on earth in that which was false; and for that ye were elated with immoderate joy. Enter ye the gates of hell, to remain therein for ever: and wretched shall be the abode of the haughty!

Wherefore persevere with patience, O Mohammed; for the promise of GOD is true. Whether we cause thee to see any part of the punishment with which we have threatened them, or whether we cause thee to die before thou see it; before us shall they be assembled at the last day. We have sent a great number of Apostles before thee; the histories of some of whom we have related unto thee, and the histories of others of them we have not related unto thee: but no apostle had the power to produce a sign, unless by the permission of GOD. When the command of GOD, therefore, shall come, judgement shall be given with truth; and then shall they perish who endeavour to render the signs of GOD of no effect.

It is GOD who hath given you the cattle, that ye may ride on some of them, and may eat of others of them (ye also receive other advantages therefrom); and that on them ye may arrive at the business proposed in your mind: and on them are ye carried by land, and on ships by sea. And he showeth you his signs: which, therefore, of the signs of GOD will ye deny? Do they not pass through the earth, and see what hath been the end of those who were before them? They were more numerous than these, and more mighty in strength, and left more considerable monuments of their power in the earth: yet that which they had acquired profited them not.

And when their apostles came unto them with evident proofs of their mission, they rejoiced in the knowledge which was with them: but that which they mocked at encompassed them. And when they beheld our vengeance, they said, We believe in GOD alone, and we renounce the idols which we associated with Him: but their faith availed them not, after they had beholden our vengeance. This was the ordinance of GOD, which was formerly observed in respect to his servants: and then did the unbelievers perish.

THE BAHÁ'Í FAITH

The Bahá'í Faith is a very recent but already widespread religious movement that has earned its place among the world's great independent religions. It was founded by Bahá'u'lláh (1817-92) who taught that He was the latest in a long succession of Messengers of God. From the very beginnings of His ministry in Persia (present-day Iran) He was fiercely opposed by the religious and political leaders of His day and was repeatedly exiled and imprisoned over a period of forty years until His passing.

The last of these exiles brought Him to the prison citadel of ʻAkká, which today is in Israel. Here His oppressors hoped that He would die, but through His benevolent influence His confinement was gradually relaxed enabling Him to take up residence outside the city's fortress walls. Although He was still considered a prisoner when He passed away, He did not regard His troubles as a hindrance to His Cause but, rather, presented the success and spread of His Cause, despite persecution, as proof of its divine origin, transcendence and spiritual power.

Many of His followers were also persecuted and large numbers of them were put to death. This section of *Accents of God* is from a book, or epistle, addressed to a man by the name of Muḥammad-Taqí. He was the son of a man responsible for the murder of two well-known and much loved followers of Baháʼuʼlláh.* Muḥammad-Taqí followed in the path of his father,

---

*Their deaths were instigated by Mírzá Muḥammad-Husayn, ʻwho, in view of a large debt he had incurred in his transactions with them, schemed to nullify his obligations by denouncing them as Bábís [i.e., followers of the Báb], and thereby encompassing their death. Their richly-furnished houses were plundered, all their remaining possessions were confiscated; Shaykh Muḥammad-Báqir, denounced by Baháʼuʼlláh as the "wolf", pronounced their death-sentence; the Zillu's-Sultán ratified the decision, after which they were put in chains, decapitated, dragged to the Maydán-i-Sháh, and there exposed to the indignities heaped upon them by a degraded and rapacious populace. "In such wise", ʻAbduʼl-Bahá [Baháʼuʼlláh's son] has written, "was the blood of these two brothers shed that the Christian priest of Julfa cried out, lamented and wept on that day." For several years Baháʼuʼlláh in His Tablets continued to make mention of them, to voice His grief over their passing and to extol their virtues' (Shoghi Effendi, *God Passes By* 200-1).

both in that he was a religious leader, or Shaykh*, and that he was persecuting followers of the new Faith. He personally trampled the corpse of one of Bahá'u'lláh's martyred followers under the feet of his horse, and was later responsible for the deaths of many Bahá'ís.

In this epistle to the Shaykh, Bahá'u'lláh calls attention to the transitory nature of the goals the Shaykh is pursuing, and encourages him to turn instead to the eternal realm of God. Throughout the epistle He quotes some of His own best known writings to acquaint the Shaykh with the true nature of His teachings and demonstrate that they never warranted the persecution He and His followers had received. He calls on the Shaykh to repent of his acts and, in setting forth His teachings, presents proofs intended to establish the validity and divine inspiration of His Cause.

Since this epistle or book was addressed to the son of a religious leader whom Bahá'u'lláh had denounced as a 'wolf', the book is appropriately entitled the *Lawḥ-i-Ibn-i-Dhi'b* meaning *The Epistle to the Son of the Wolf.* It is Bahá'u'lláh's last major work and, in effect, can be viewed as His own summary of His central religious teachings. As such, it provides an excellent text for anyone wishing to contemplate or seek to understand Bahá'u'lláh's teachings. Indeed, it is unlikely that its intended audience was merely one individual. When reading the text it becomes clear that, as with many of His writings, while addressing a particular individual its message is applicable to all of humanity. Bahá'u'lláh

---

*A proponent of a specific sect of Shí'ah Islam

Himself wrote: 'The summons and the message which We gave were never intended to reach one land or one people only' (*Tablets of Bahá'u'lláh* 89).*

When Bahá'u'lláh speaks to the 'son of the wolf', He is addressing the dark side in all of us. When He calls the Shaykh to repentance and to take up the spiritual path, He is calling us to the divine that lies within us all. Here, in a sense, is the eternal voice of the Lord of Hosts, calling out to us across the battlefield of our own personal Armageddon, calling us away from the enemy lines of hatred and our own selfish interests to the victory that the spiritual life holds for us.

The particular selection chosen follows the opening portion of the book that calls upon the Shaykh to change his ways. It introduces Bahá'u'lláh's claim to revealed truth and then takes up one of the most central precepts of His teachings, the unity of the world's different religions. This selection is especially appropriate for a book like *Accents of God* because it asserts and expounds on the oneness of religion by explaining why the religions differ and re-stating their common primal spiritual purpose and true aim. Although He praises the conduct of religious leaders who are sincere, He seeks to eliminate the evil of religious fanaticism by emphasizing how many religious leaders, instead of guiding the believers to God, have instilled fanaticism and prejudice into the hearts of their followers, thus turning religion against its own purpose.

---

* That the *Lawḥ-i-Ibn-i-Dhi'b* is not solely directed to the Shaykh is also suggested by several instances where Bahá'u'lláh makes statements in the text which He directs to the 'people of Bahá', meaning His followers.

Bahá'u'lláh is here calling us back to religion's original intent and purpose, the promotion of 'the knowledge of God' and the furthering of 'unity and fellowship' among the peoples of the world. By setting forth teachings about the fundamental unity existing between the world's religions, Bahá'u'lláh outlines a path of religious tolerance and appreciation. Because contact between the world's different religions has now become an everyday occurrence, this path is essential to the leading of a spiritual life in this day. It helps us live our lives in a way that brings about harmony and reflects the divine love that embraces all people.

❊

WE BESEECH GOD TO AID THEE to be just and fair-minded, and to acquaint thee with the things that were hidden from the eyes of men. He, in truth, is the Mighty, the Unconstrained. We ask thee to reflect upon that which hath been revealed, and to be fair and just in thy speech, that perchance the splendours of the day-star of truthfulness and sincerity may shine forth, and may deliver thee from the darkness of ignorance, and illumine the world with the light of knowledge. This Wronged One [Bahá'u'lláh] hath frequented no school, neither hath He attended the controversies of the learned. By My life! Not of Mine own volition have I revealed Myself, but God, of His own choosing, hath manifested Me. In the Tablet, addressed to His Majesty the Shah* - may God, blessed and glorified be He, assist him - these words have streamed from the tongue of this Wronged One:

> 'O King! I was but a man like others, asleep upon My
> couch, when lo, the breezes of the All-Glorious were
> wafted over Me, and taught Me the knowledge of all
> that hath been. This thing is not from Me, but from

*The ruler of Persia (Iran), Náṣiri'd-Dín Sháh (1848-96).

One Who is Almighty and All-Knowing. And He bade Me lift up My voice between earth and heaven, and for this there befell Me what hath caused the tears of every man of understanding to flow. The learning current amongst men I studied not; their schools I entered not. Ask of the city wherein I dwelt, that thou mayest be well assured that I am not of them who speak falsely. This is but a leaf which the winds of the will of thy Lord, the Almighty, the All-Praised, have stirred. Can it be still when the tempestuous winds are blowing? Nay, by Him Who is the Lord of all Names and Attributes! They move it as they list. The evanescent is as nothing before Him Who is the Ever-Abiding. His all-compelling summons hath reached Me, and caused Me to speak His praise amidst all people. I was indeed as one dead when His behest was uttered. The hand of the will of thy Lord, the Compassionate, the Merciful, transformed Me*.'

Now is the moment in which to cleanse thyself with the waters of detachment that have flowed out from the Supreme Pen, and to ponder, wholly for the sake of God, those things which, time and again, have been sent down or manifested, and then to strive, as much as lieth in thee, to quench, through the power of wisdom and the force of thy utterance, the fire of enmity and

---

*With reference to a similar passage, Bahá'u'lláh's son, 'Abdu'l-Bahá, explained that such statements are metaphorical and should not be understood to mean literally that Bahá'u'lláh or any Prophet of God was not always in a state of Prophethood. See 'Abdu'l-Bahá, *Some Answered Questions*, ch. 16.

hatred which smouldereth in the hearts of the peoples of the world. The Divine Messengers[*] have been sent down, and their Books were revealed, for the purpose of promoting the knowledge of God, and of furthering unity and fellowship amongst men. But now behold, how they have made the Law of God a cause and pretext for perversity and hatred. How pitiful, how regrettable, that most men are cleaving fast to, and have busied themselves with, the things they possess, and are unaware of, and shut out as by a veil from, the things God possesseth!

Say: 'O God, my God! Attire mine head with the crown of justice, and my temple with the ornament of equity. Thou, verily, art the Possessor of all gifts and bounties.'

Justice and equity are twin Guardians that watch over men. From them are revealed such blessed and perspicuous words as are the cause of the well-being of the world and the protection of the nations.

These words have streamed from the pen of this Wronged One in one of His Tablets:

> 'The purpose of the one true God, exalted be His glory, hath been to bring forth the Mystic Gems out of the mine of man - they Who are the Dawning-Places of His Cause and the Repositories of the pearls of His knowledge; for, God Himself, glorified be He, is the Unseen, the One concealed and hidden from the eyes of

---

[*] That is, Moses, Christ, Muḥammad and others.

men. Consider what the Merciful hath revealed in the Qur'án: No vision taketh in Him, but He taketh in all vision, and He is the Subtle, the All-Informed!'*

That the divers communions of the earth, and the manifold systems of religious belief, should never be allowed to foster the feelings of animosity among men, is, in this Day, of the essence of the Faith of God and His Religion. These principles and laws, these firmly-established and mighty systems, have proceeded from one Source, and are rays of one Light. That they differ one from another is to be attributed to the varying requirements of the ages in which they were promulgated.

Gird up the loins of your endeavour, O people of Bahá,§ that haply the tumult of religious dissension and strife that agitateth the peoples of the earth may be stilled, that every trace of it may be completely obliterated. For the love of God, and them that serve Him, arise to aid this sublime and momentous Revelation. Religious fanaticism and hatred are a world-devouring fire, whose violence none can quench. The Hand of Divine power can, alone, deliver mankind from this desolating affliction. Consider the war** that hath involved the two Nations, how both sides have renounced their possessions and their lives. How many the villages that were completely wiped out!

The utterance of God is a lamp, whose light are these words: Ye are the fruits of one tree, and the leaves of one branch. Deal ye

---

*Qur'án 6:103.
§Meaning the followers of Bahá'u'lláh.
**Possibly a reference to the earlier Crimean War.

one with another with the utmost love and harmony, with friendliness and fellowship. He Who is the Day-Star of Truth beareth Me witness! So powerful is the light of unity that it can illuminate the whole earth. The One true God, He Who knoweth all things, Himself testifieth to the truth of these words.

Exert yourselves that ye may attain this transcendent and most sublime station, the station that can insure the protection and security of all mankind. This goal excelleth every other goal, and this aspiration is the monarch of all aspirations. So long, however, as the thick clouds of oppression, which obscure the day-star of justice, remain undispelled, it would be difficult for the glory of this station to be unveiled to men's eyes. These thick clouds are the exponents of idle fancies and vain imaginings, who are none other but the divines of Persia. At one time We spoke in the language of the lawgiver; at another in that of the truth-seeker and the mystic, and yet Our supreme purpose and highest wish hath always been to disclose the glory and sublimity of this station. God, verily, is a sufficient witness!

Consort with all men, O people of Bahá, in a spirit of friendliness and fellowship. If ye be aware of a certain truth, if ye possess a jewel, of which others are deprived, share it with them in a language of utmost kindliness and good-will. If it be accepted, if it fulfil its purpose, your object is attained. If anyone should refuse it, leave him unto himself, and beseech God to guide him. Beware lest ye deal unkindly with him. A kindly tongue is the lodestone of the hearts of men. It is the bread of the spirit, it clotheth the words with meaning, it is the fountain of the light of wisdom and understanding.

By 'divines' in the passage cited above is meant those men who outwardly attire themselves with the raiment of knowledge, but who inwardly are deprived therefrom. In this connection, We quote from the Tablet addressed to His Majesty the Sháh, certain passages from the 'Hidden Words' which were revealed by the Abhá Pen under the name of the 'Book of Fáṭimih,' the blessings of God be upon her!*

> 'O ye that are foolish, yet have a name to be wise! Wherefore do ye wear the guise of the shepherd, when inwardly ye have become wolves, intent upon My flock? Ye are even as the star, which riseth ere the dawn, and which, though it seem radiant and luminous, leadeth the wayfarers of My city astray into the paths of perdition.'

And likewise He saith:

> 'O ye seeming fair yet inwardly foul! Ye are like clear but bitter water, which to outward seeming is crystal pure but of which, when tested by the Divine Assayer, not a drop is accepted. Yea, the sunbeam falls alike upon the dust and the mirror, yet differ they in reflection even

*Fáṭimih was the daughter of Muḥammad. In the sayings of Shí'ah Islam, there is an allegory which says that when her husband 'Alí, the successor of Muḥammad, died, the angel Gabriel descended upon her and spoke certain words of consolation to her. These words are said to compose a mystical book, the *Book of Fáṭimih*. Bahá'u'lláh's book, *The Hidden Words*, is here associated with this allegorical work.

as doth the star from the earth: nay, immeasurable is the difference!'

And also He saith:

> 'O essence of desire! At many a dawn have I turned from the realms of the Placeless unto thine abode, and found thee on the bed of ease busied with others than Myself. Thereupon, even as the flash of the spirit, I returned to the realms of celestial glory, and breathed it not in My retreats above unto the hosts of holiness.'

And again He saith:

> 'O bond slave of the world! Many a dawn hath the breeze of My loving-kindness wafted over thee and found thee upon the bed of heedlessness fast asleep. Bewailing then thy plight it returned whence it came.'

Those divines, however, who are truly adorned with the ornament of knowledge and of a goodly character are, verily, as a head to the body of the world, and as eyes to the nations. The guidance of men hath, at all times, been, and is, dependent upon such blessed souls. We beseech God to graciously aid them to do His will and pleasure. He, in truth, is the Lord of all men, the Lord of this world and of the next.

O Shaykh! We have learned that thou hast turned away from Us, and protested against Us, in such wise that thou hast bidden the people to curse Me, and decreed that the blood of the servants of God be shed. God requite him who said: 'Willingly will I obey the judge who hath so strangely decreed that my blood be spilt at Ḥill and at Ḥaram!' Verily I say: Whatever befalleth in the path of God is the beloved of the soul and the desire of the heart. Deadly poison in His path is pure honey, and every tribulation a draught of crystal water. In the Tablet to His Majesty the S͟háh it is written: 'By Him Who is the Truth! I fear no tribulation in His path, nor any affliction in My love for Him. Verily God hath made adversity as a morning dew upon His green pasture, and a wick for His lamp which lighteth earth and heaven.'

Set thine heart towards Him Who is the Ka‘bah* of God, the Help in Peril, the Self-Subsisting, and raise thou thine hands with such firm conviction as shall cause the hands of all created things to be lifted up towards the heaven of the grace of God, the Lord of all worlds. Turn, then, thy face towards Him in such wise that the faces of all beings will turn in the direction of His shining and luminous Horizon, and say:

'Thou seest me, O my Lord, with my face turned towards the heaven of Thy bounty and the ocean of Thy favour, withdrawn from all else beside Thee. I ask of Thee, by the splendours of the Sun of Thy revelation on Sinai, and the effulgences of the Orb of Thy grace which shineth from the horizon of Thy Name, the Ever-

---

*In Bahá'u'lláh's writings the Ka‘bah signifies the place where He, the Manifestation, is present. It signifies the presence of God on earth and the place of atonement, even as the Jerusalem Temple in the ancient Jewish Faith. In Islam the term specifically refers to a cube-shaped building in Mecca.

Forgiving, to grant me Thy pardon and to have mercy upon me. Write down, then, for me with Thy pen of glory that which will exalt me through Thy Name in the world of creation. Aid me, O my Lord, to set myself towards Thee, and to hearken unto the voice of Thy loved ones, whom the powers of the earth have failed to weaken, and the dominion of the nations has been powerless to withhold from Thee, and who, advancing towards Thee, have said: "God is our Lord, the Lord of all who are in heaven and all who are on earth!" '

O Shaykh! Verily I say, the seal of the Choice Wine hath, in the name of Him Who is the Self-Subsisting, been broken; withhold not thyself therefrom. This Wronged One speaketh wholly for the sake of God; thou too shouldst, likewise, for the sake of God, meditate upon those things that have been sent down and manifested, that haply thou mayest, on this blessed Day, take thy portion of the liberal effusions of Him Who is truly the All-Bountiful, and mayest not remain deprived thereof. This indeed would not be hard for God. Dust-made Adam* was raised up, through the Word of God, to the heavenly throne, and a mere fisherman§ was made the repository of Divine wisdom, and Abú-Dhar**, the shepherd, became a prince of the nations!

This Day, O Shaykh, hath never been, nor is it now, the Day whereon man-made arts and sciences can be regarded as a true

---

*A reference to the symbolism of Genesis 2:7.
§Meaning St Peter (Mark 1:16; Matthew 16:13–19).
**An illiterate shepherd who became an esteemed disciple of Muḥammad.

standard for men, since it hath been recognized that He Who was wholly unversed in any of them hath ascended the throne of purest gold, and occupied the seat of honour in the council of knowledge, whilst the acknowledged exponent and repository of these arts and sciences remained utterly deprived. By 'arts and sciences' is meant those which begin with words and end with words. Such arts and sciences, however, as are productive of good results, and bring forth their fruit, and are conducive to the well-being and tranquility of men have been, and will remain, acceptable before God. Wert thou to give ear to My voice, thou wouldst cast away all thy possessions, and wouldst set thy face towards the Spot wherein the ocean of wisdom and of utterance hath surged, and the sweet savours of the loving-kindness of thy Lord, the Compassionate, have wafted.

PHOTO GLOSSARY

Page 9:

This picture is of Ayers Rock which rises 348 metres above the surrounding desert plain in the Northern Territory of Australia. Known to the aborgines as 'Uluru', it is an ancient religious site sacred to many tribes. The caves at its base contain symbolic carvings and paintings. (Photo: Tony Stone Photolibrary, no. W17L 247605-1P)

Page 15:

This plain at Kuruksetra, about 120 kilometres north-west of Delhi, India, is believed to be the site where the opposing armies described in the opening chapter of the Bhagavad-gita gathered to engage in combat. Here, tradition says, Krishna spoke the immortal words of the Bhagavad-gita to His friend, the warrior Arjuna. The place is held in great reverence by many Hindus and is a place of pilgrimage. (Photo: courtesy of the Bhaktivendata Trust)

Page 29:

The Monastery of St Catherine, shown in this photo, is adjacent to a mountain which, according to some traditions, is Mount Sinai where the Law was revealed by God to Moses. This monastery, in the Sinai Desert of Egypt, was built at the instruction of Emperor Justinian in the sixth century. It was constructed, according to early accounts, around what was believed to be the Burning Bush in which God first spoke to Moses (Exodus 3:1-4:17). (Photo: Tony Stone Photolibrary, e5011 510330-1P)

Page 37:

The remains of the Great Stupa of Sarnath. This site is located about 10 kilometres from the holy city of Varanasi on the River Ganges, India. It was here that Buddha first preached His teachings concerning the four noble truths and the path to Nirvana. Later, the Buddhist emperor Asoka erected majestic stupas here to honour the sacred site. (Photo: Stepanie Colasanti, no. 876)

Page 49:

The Mount of Beatitudes is located on the north-western shore of the Sea of Galilee, Israel. For Christians this is one of the holiest sites in all Israel, being the place where, according to tradition, Jesus delivered the Sermon on the Mount. The Church was built in 1936 by the Associazione Italiane and is run by the Franciscan Sisters of the Immaculate Heart of Mary. (Photo: Stepanie Colasanti, no. 689)

Page 61:

The holy city of Mecca, Saudi Arabia. The photo shows the Muslim shrine, the Ka'bah, which is the main place of pilgrimage for Muslims. According to tradition the original Ka'bah was founded by Adam and later rebuilt by Abraham. Before the time of Muḥammad, the Ka'bah had been turned into a shrine for various idols. Muḥammad captured Mecca and removed the idols. The Ka'bah was then once again restored as a place of pilgrimage and worship of God. (Photo: Tony Stone Photolibrary, no. V72L 268075-6A)

Page 75:

The Mansion of Bahjí, meaning 'place of delight', in 'Akká, Israel, was the last place of residence of Bahá'u'lláh. It was here that He revealed the *Lawḥ-i-Ibn-i-Dhi'b*. This mansion was abandoned in 1879 when the Khammár family fled the site due to an outbreak of an epidemic disease. Bahá'u'lláh's son, 'Abdu'l-Bahá, first rented and later purchased the mansion for His Father where He resided - still technically a prisoner - from 1879 until His passing in 1892. Bahá'u'lláh was buried in the small house adjacent to the Mansion and it is the main place of pilgrimage for Bahá'ís throughout the world. The Mansion later underwent restoration and in the early 1950s a programme of beautification began which included the addition of extensive gardens. The mansion is regarded as a symbol of Bahá'u'lláh's triumph over the many years of persecution He suffered.   (Photo courtesy of Audio-Visual Department of the Bahá'í World Centre, Haifa, Israel)

ONEWORLD

Books for Thoughtful People

———

If you would like to receive our mail order catalogue and be
placed on our mailing list for regular updates on our current
and forthcoming titles, please write to the address below.

Oneworld Publications
185 Banbury Road
Oxford, OX2 7AR
England